New Seasons is a trademark of Publications International, Ltd.

Louis Weber, CEO
Publications International, Ltd.
7373 North Cicero Avenue
Lincolnwood, Illinois 60712

www.pilbooks.com

Manufactured in China.

8 7 6 5 4 3 2 1

ISBN: 1-4127-4778-3

Hey Girlfriend

Girls Will Be Girls!

new seasons™

Everyone knows about the Wright brothers, but very few people know about their sister Daphne.

"This is the best prison break *ever!*"

Later, all they would find of the Benson twins were the bathing caps and some shreds of orange plastic.

Joanna and Julia really did party 'til the cows came home.

If you think these are cool you should have seen the drinks they came in.

Aunt Alice took credit for inventing the all-purpose protest sign.

WE'RE RIGHT!

A tattoo should *not* be an impulse buy.

Double-dating can lead to unique and exciting experiences.

MISS NUT TREE

The runner-up was bitterly disappointed, but even she had to admit, Miss Nut Tree sure had a lot of teeth.

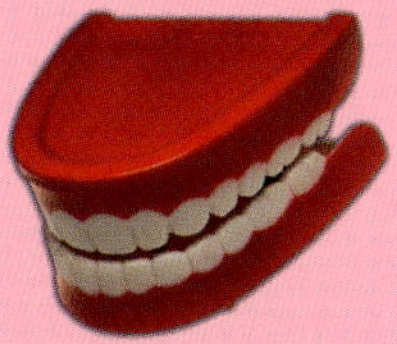

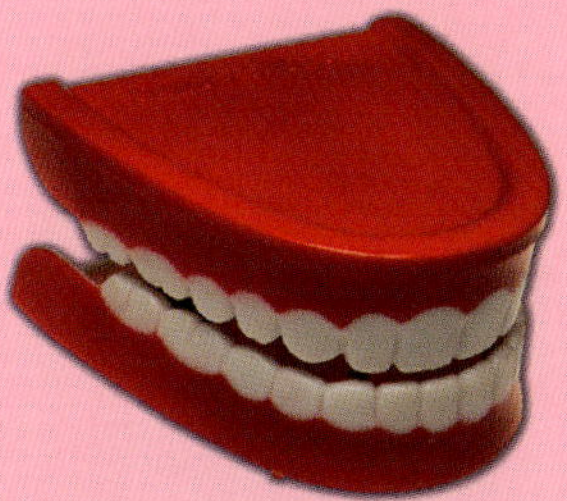

Nothing starts a workday like snap, crackle, and pop.

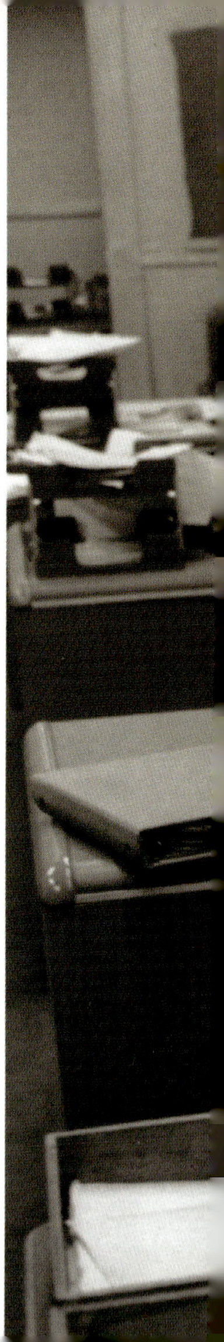

"Yes, it's handy. Now please take it back to the store and get the earrings I asked for."

"Eat my pumps!"

"And they say *women* are bad drivers!"

Some days Patty really was the brightest bulb in the box.

If we liked Melissa better we would have said something.

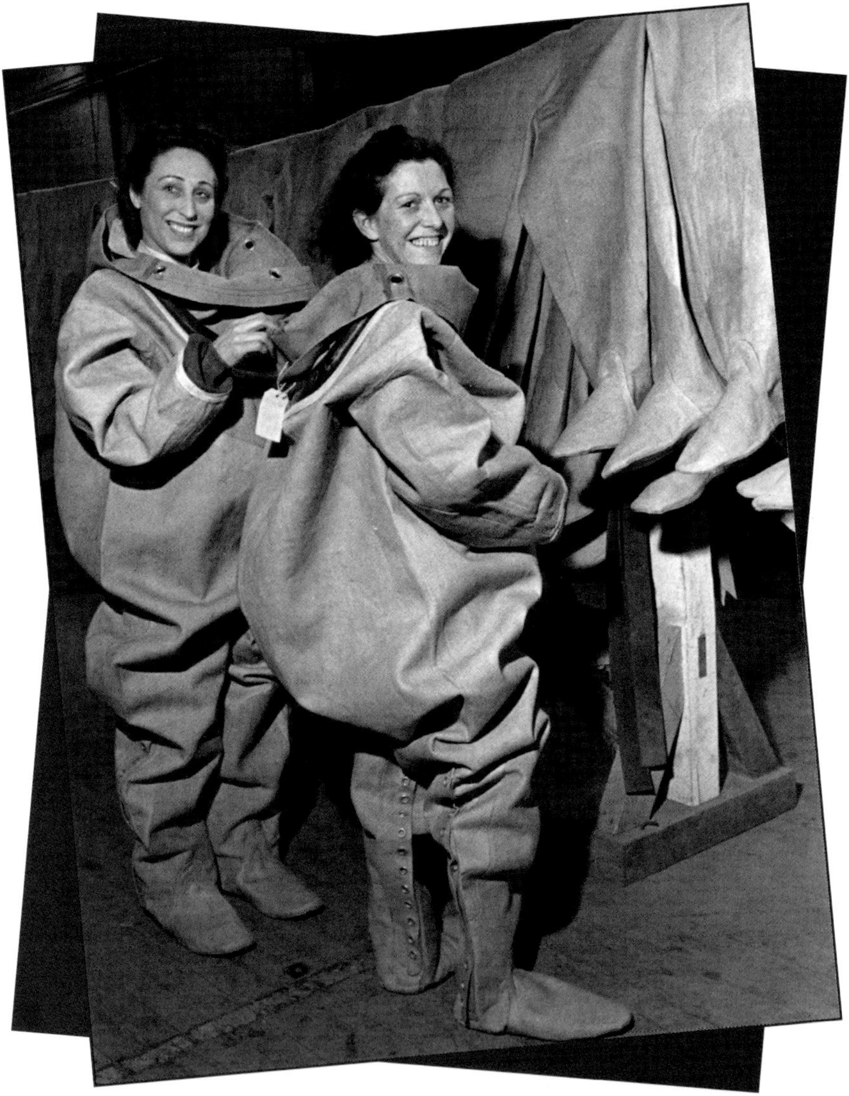

"Does this outfit make me look fat?"

It is a
little-known fact
that beauty
pageants used to
be decided by a
battle royale.

"They're fun at first—
but after a while, it's
just a lot of dirty
newspaper."

"Umm, Linda, you need to turn a little more to your left, and Mary, I think you're out of position too."

Judy and Diane had finally invented the perfect man: tall, strong, and always does what he's told.

There are brides, and then there are Bridezillas.

"I knew I should have worn my push-up bra."

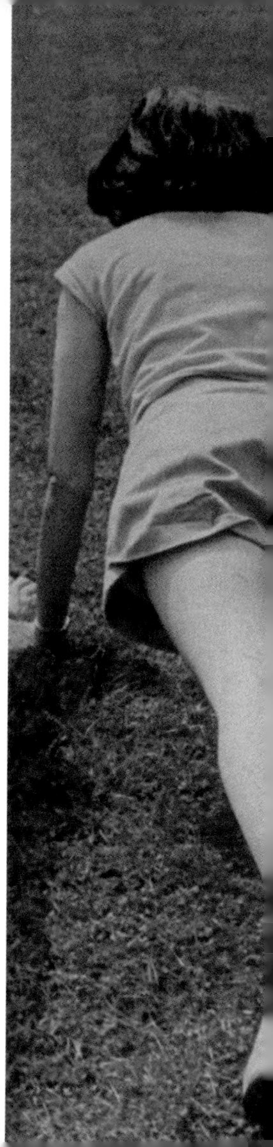

Sue claimed to be the inventor of wireless communication.

And that's when they realized that the hokey pokey IS what it's all about.

"When I find a guy who doesn't mind seeing me in these, I'll know he's 'The One.'"

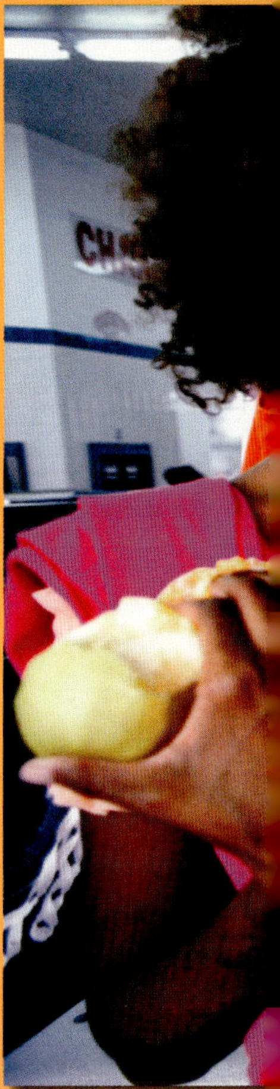

"Doctor, what did you say the side effects of Botox™ were again?"

"I can't hold this position much longer. Have those guys noticed us yet?"

Who says only jokers are wild?

Walking your dog in the park is a great way to attract men. And, as the girls discovered, a great way to scare them off.

Unfortunately for Edith Mae, it would be years before the invention of the sports bra.

Molly wore her heart on her sleeve and her produce on her head.

Climbing the corporate ladder is almost as fun as going down the corporate slide.

Looking for love in all the wrong places.

Fences make good neighbors. Short fences make great neighbors.

"That's the last time I let you talk me into playing poker."

Riding off into the sunset was going to be more difficult than they thought.

Photography credits:

Front cover: **Taxi/Getty Images**

Back cover: **Hulton Archive/Getty Images**

Getty Images: Hulton Archive, 12–13, 14, 17, 21, 25, 30–31, 36, 38–39, 45, 52, 58–59, 62–63, 65, 70, 74, 76–77; The Image Bank, 6–7, 8–9, 29, 42–43, 57, 73; Taxi, 10, 22, 32, 46, 51, 54–55, 60–61, 67, 68; Time Life Pictures, 26, 48–49; **ImageState:** Patti McConville, 35; StockImage, 18, 40